Piano • Vocal • Guitar

2nd EDITION

The BIG BAND Era

T0084228

ISBN-13: 978-1-4234-2403-1
ISBN-10: 1-4234-2403-4

HAL•LEONARD® CORPORATION
7777 W. BLUEMOUND RD. P.O.BOX 13819 MILWAUKEE, WI 53213

Visit Hal Leonard Online at
www.halleonard.com

Contents

AC-CENT-TCHU-ATE THE POSITIVE

from the Motion Picture HERE COME THE WAVES

Lyric by JOHNNY MERCER
Music by HAROLD ARLEN

Moderately

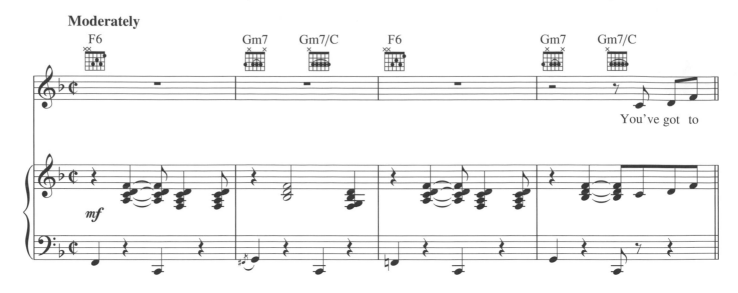

You've got to

ac - cent - tchu-ate the pos - i - tive, e - lim - i - nate the neg - a - tive, __

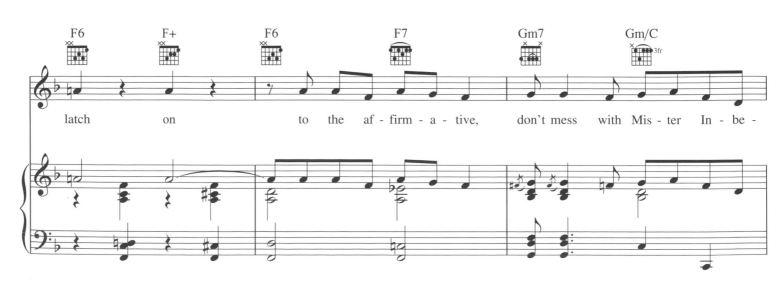

latch   on   to the af - firm - a - tive,   don't mess   with Mis - ter   In - be -

ACROSS THE ALLEY
FROM THE ALAMO

Words and Music by
JOE GREENE

ALL OF ME

Words and Music by SEYMOUR SIMONS
and GERALD MARKS

BETWEEN THE DEVIL AND THE DEEP BLUE SEA

from RHYTHMANIA

Lyric by TED KOEHLER
Music by HAROLD ARLEN

BOO-HOO

*Lyric and Music by EDWARD HEYMAN,
CARMEN LOMBARDO and JOHN JACOB LOEB*

BOOGIE WOOGIE BUGLE BOY
from BUCK PRIVATES

Words and Music by DON RAYE
and HUGHIE PRINCE

THE BREEZE AND I

Words by AL STILLMAN
Music by ERNESTO LECUONA

BYE BYE BLUES

Words and Music by FRED HAMM, DAVE BENNETT
BERT LOWN and CHAUNCEY GRAY

CHEROKEE
(Indian Love Song)

Words and Music by
RAY NOBLE

one day I'll hold you,

in my arms fold you,

Cher - o - kee.

kee.

CIRIBIRIBIN

Based on the original melody by A. PESTALOZZA
English version by HARRY JAMES
and JACK LAWRENCE

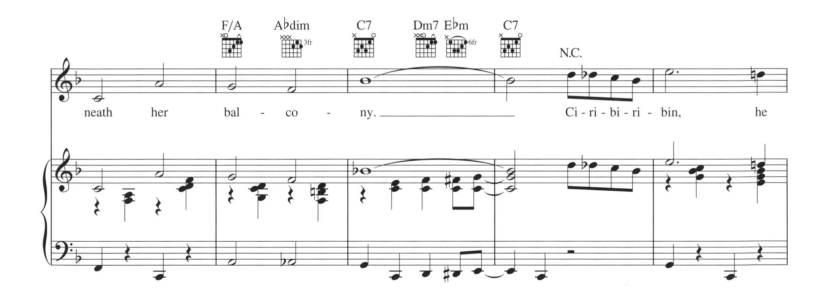

DARN THAT DREAM

Lyric by EDDIE DE LANGE
Music by JIMMY VAN HEUSEN

DO NOTHIN' TILL YOU HEAR FROM ME

Words and Music by DUKE ELLINGTON
and BOB RUSSELL

DON'T SIT UNDER THE APPLE TREE
(With Anyone Else but Me)

Words and Music by LEW BROWN,
SAM H. STEPT and CHARLIE TOBIAS

EAST OF THE SUN
(And West of the Moon)

Words and Music by
BROOKS BOWMAN

HARBOR LIGHTS

Words and Music by JIMMY KENNEDY
and HUGH WILLIAMS

EVERYTHING HAPPENS TO ME

Words by TOM ADAIR
Music by MATT DENNIS

Black cats creep a-cross my path un-til I'm al-most mad, I must have 'roused the dev-il's wrath 'cause all my luck is bad. I make a date for golf and you can bet your life it rains, I

FIVE FOOT TWO, EYES OF BLUE
(Has Anybody Seen My Girl?)

Words by JOE YOUNG and SAM LEWIS
Music by RAY HENDERSON

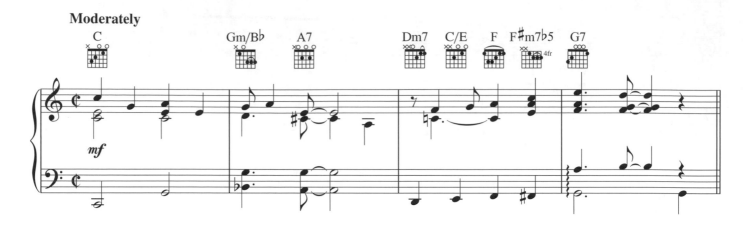

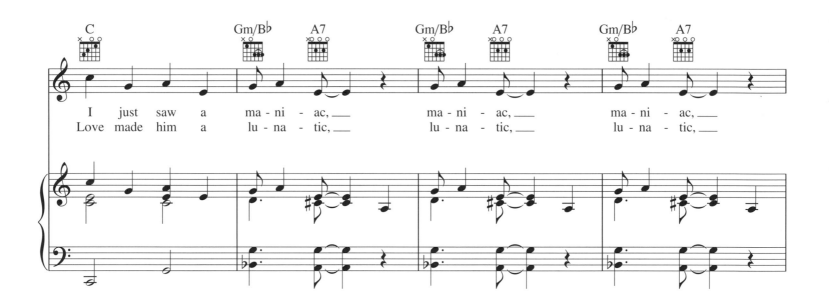

I just saw a ma-ni-ac, __ ma-ni-ac, __ ma-ni-ac, __
Love made him a lu-na-tic, __ lu-na-tic, __ lu-na-tic, __

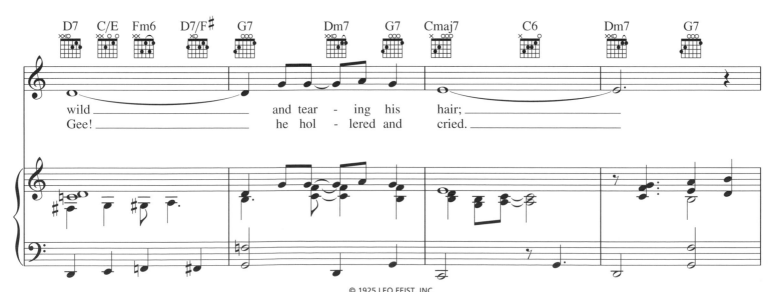

wild _____ and tear-ing his hair; _____
Gee! _____ he hol-lered and cried.

FLAT FOOT FLOOGIE

Words and Music by SLIM GAILLARD,
SLAM STEWART and BUD GREEN

HERE'S THAT RAINY DAY
from CARNIVAL IN FLANDERS

Words by JOHNNY BURKE
Music by JIMMY VAN HEUSEN

HONEYSUCKLE ROSE
from AIN'T MISBEHAVIN'

Words by ANDY RAZAF
Music by THOMAS "FATS" WALLER

HEY! BA-BA-RE-BOP

Words and Music by LIONEL HAMPTON
and CURLEY HAMMER

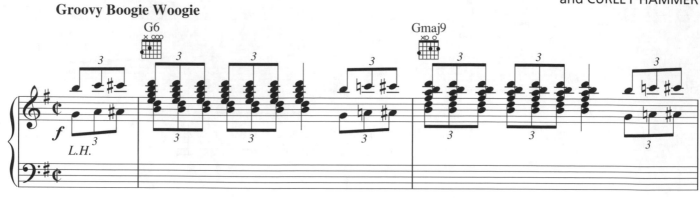

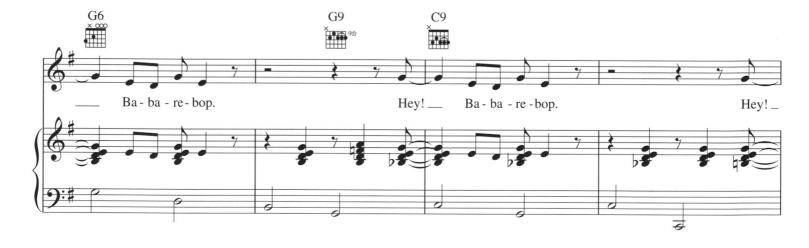

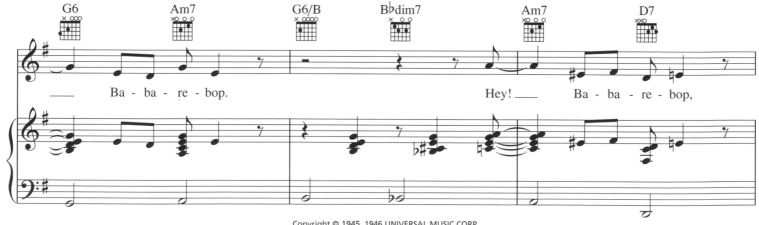

HOW HIGH THE MOON

from TWO FOR THE SHOW

Words by NANCY HAMILTON
Music by MORGAN LEWIS

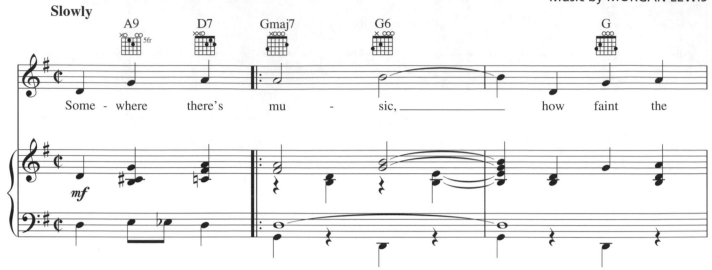

Some - where there's mu - sic, _____ how faint the

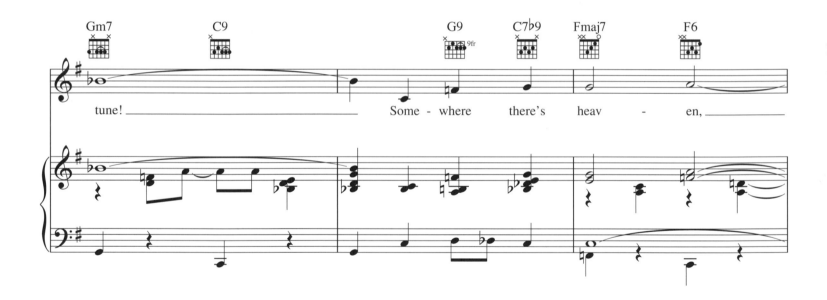

tune! _____ Some - where there's heav - en, _____

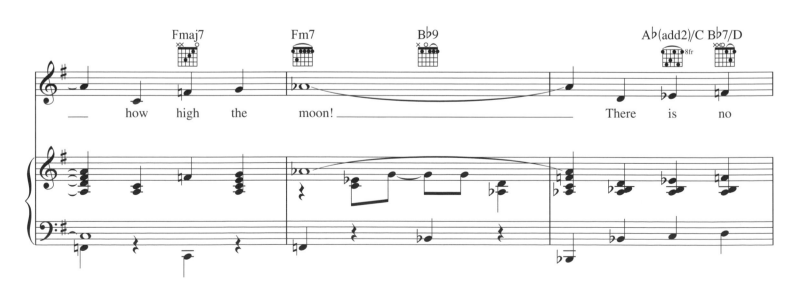

___ how high the moon! _____ There is no

I CAN DREAM, CAN'T I?

from RIGHT THIS WAY

Lyric by IRVING KAHAL
Music by SAMMY FAIN

8vb

I CAN'T GET STARTED WITH YOU

from ZIEGFELD FOLLIES

Words by IRA GERSHWIN
Music by VERNON DUKE

I'm a glum one, it's ex-plain - a - ble:

I met some-one un - at-tain - a-ble. Life's a bore, the world is my oy-ster no

more. All the pa - pers where I led the news

I CAN'T GIVE YOU ANYTHING BUT LOVE

from BLACKBIRDS OF 1928

Words and Music by JIMMY McHUGH
and DOROTHY FIELDS

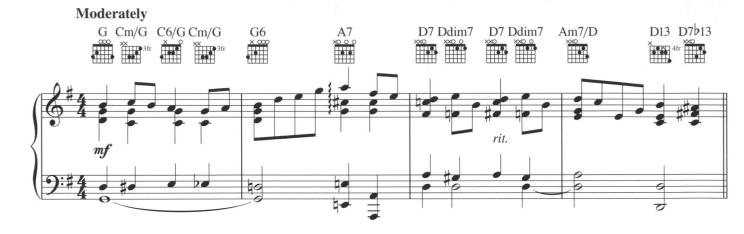

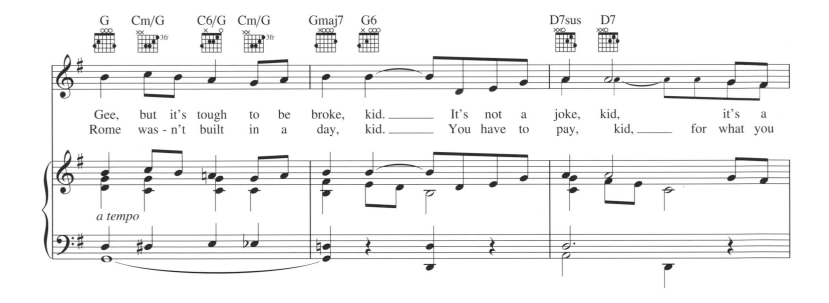

Gee, but it's tough to be broke, kid. ____ It's not a joke, kid, ____ it's a
Rome was-n't built in a day, kid. ____ You have to pay, kid, ____ for what you

curse. My luck is chang-ing, it's got-ten ____ from sim-ply
get. But I am will-ing to wait, dear; ____ your lit-tle

I DIDN'T KNOW WHAT TIME IT WAS

from TOO MANY GIRLS

Words by LORENZ HART
Music by RICHARD RODGERS

I DON'T STAND A GHOST OF A CHANCE

Words by BING CROSBY and NED WASHINGTON
Music by VICTOR YOUNG

I DON'T WANT TO SET THE WORLD ON FIRE

Words by EDDIE SEILER and SOL MARCUS
Music by BENNIE BENJAMIN and EDDIE DURHAM

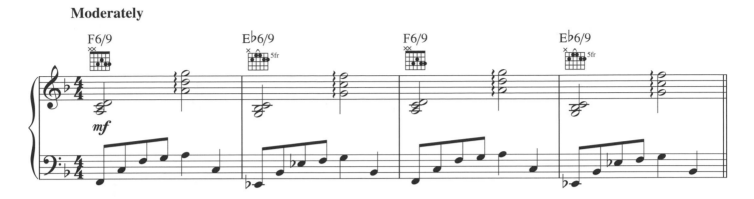

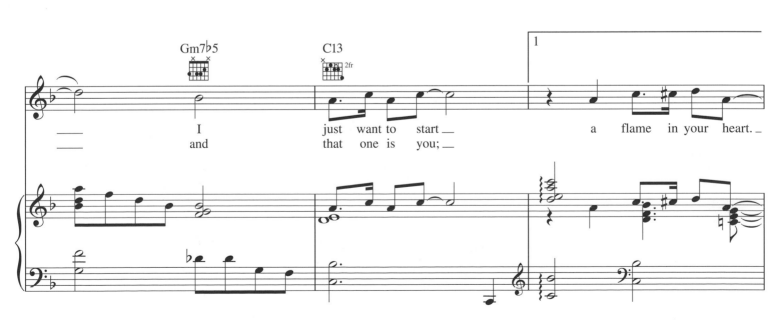

I'LL BE AROUND

Words and Music by
ALEC WILDER

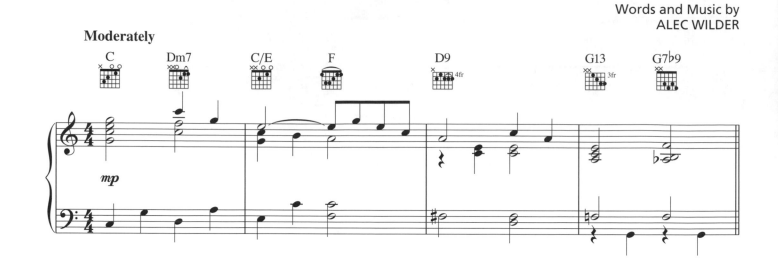

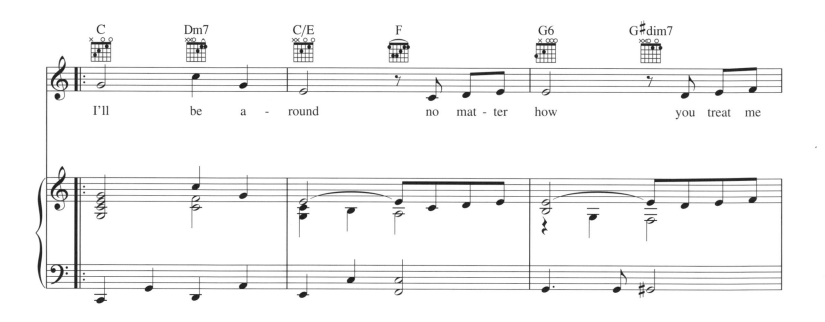

I'll   be a - round   no mat - ter how   you treat me

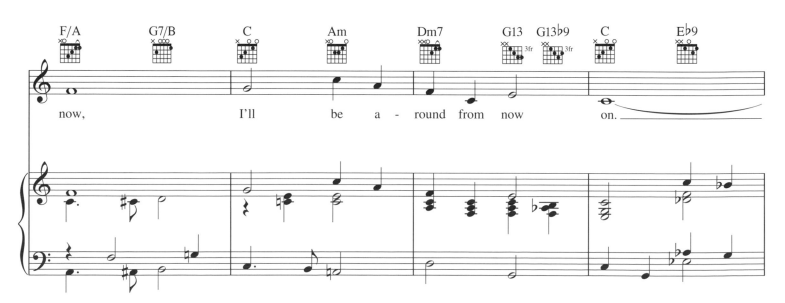

now,   I'll   be a - round from now   on.

I'LL GET BY
(As Long as I Have You)

Lyric by ROY TURK
Music by FRED E. AHLERT

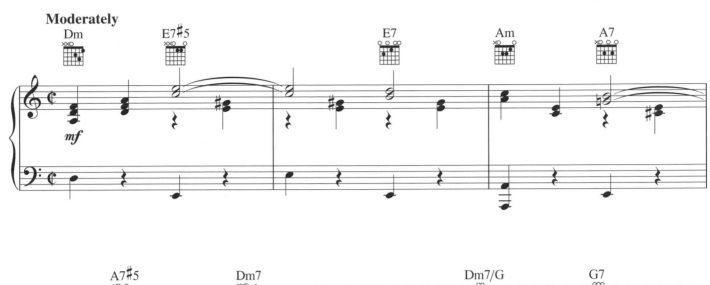

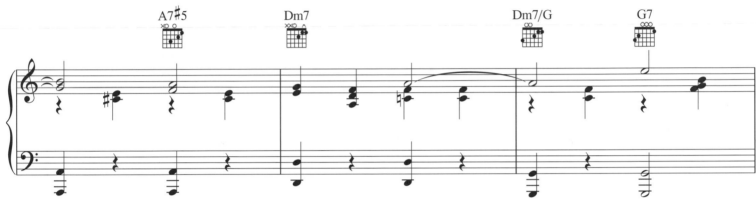

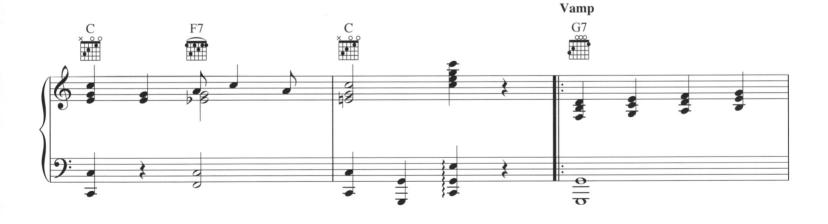

I'LL BE SEEING YOU

from RIGHT THIS WAY

Written by IRVING KAHAL
and SAMMY FAIN

Moderately

Ca-the-dral bells were toll-ing _____ And our hearts sang on, _____

__ Was it the spell of Par - is _____ Or the A - pril dawn? _____

Who knows, _____ if we shall meet a - gain?

I'LL REMEMBER APRIL

Words and Music by PAT JOHNSON,
DON RAYE and GENE DE PAUL

Moderately, with expression

This love-ly day will length-en in-to eve-ning; we'll sigh good-bye to all we've ev-er had. A-lone, where we have walked to-geth-er, I'll re-

I'M BEGINNING TO SEE THE LIGHT
featured in SOPHISTICATED LADIES

Words and Music by DON GEORGE, JOHNNY HODGES,
DUKE ELLINGTON and HARRY JAMES

Then you came and caused a spark __ that's a four a-larm fire __ now. __

__ I nev-er made love by lan-tern shine, __ I

nev-er saw rain-bows in my wine, __ but now that your lips are

burn-ing mine, __ I'm be-gin-ning to see the light. __ I __

8vb

I'M CONFESSIN'
(That I Love You)

Words and Music by AL NEIBURG,
DOC DAUGHERTY and ELLIS REYNOLDS

I'VE HEARD THAT SONG BEFORE

from the Motion Picture YOUTH ON PARADE

Lyric by SAMMY CAHN
Music by JULE STYNE

Mu - sic helps me to re - mem - ber, _____ it helps re - mind me _____ of things be - hind me. _____ Though I'm bet - ter off for - get - ting, _____ I try in

IMAGINATION

Words by JOHNNY BURKE
Music by JIMMY VAN HEUSEN

na - tion is sil - ly. You go a - round wil - ly -

nil - ly. For ex - am - ple, I go a - round want - ing

you, _____ and yet, I can't i - mag - ine that you want me

too. _____ I - mag - i - too. _____

IN A SHANTY IN OLD SHANTY TOWN

Lyric by JOE YOUNG
Music by JACK LITTLE and IRA SCHUSTER

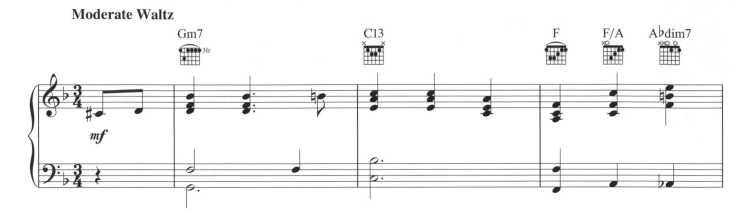

I'm up in the world, but I'd give the

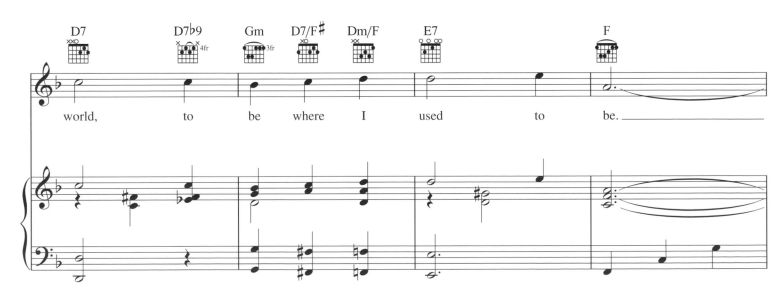

world, to be where I used to be.

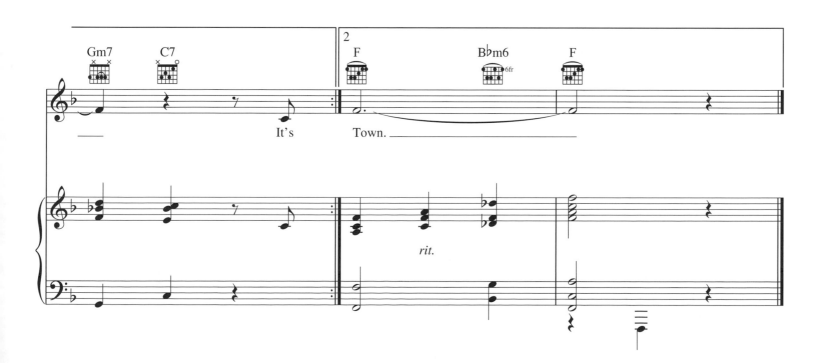

IN THE MOOD

By JOE GARLAND

INDIANA
(Back Home Again in Indiana)

Words by BALLARD MacDONALD
Music by JAMES F. HANLEY

IS YOU IS, OR IS YOU AIN'T
(Ma' Baby)
from FOLLOW THE BOYS
from FIVE GUYS NAMED MOE

Words and Music by BILLY AUSTIN
and LOUIS JORDAN

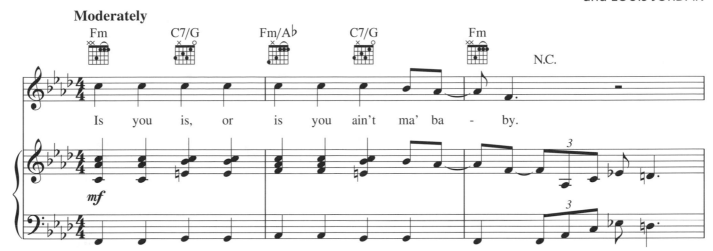

Is you is, or is you ain't ma' ba - by.

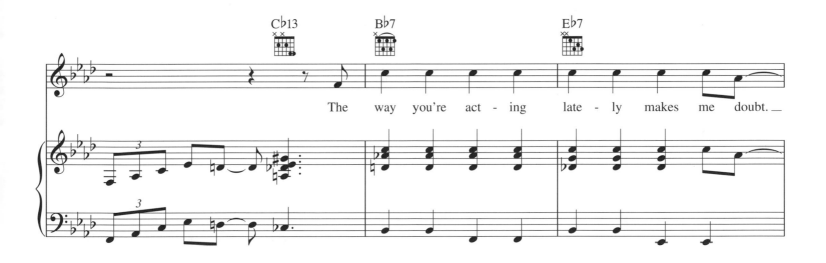

The way you're act - ing late - ly makes me doubt.

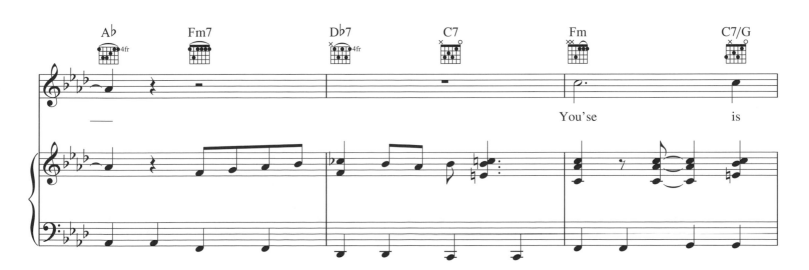

You'se is

IT'S ONLY A PAPER MOON

featured in the Motion Picture TAKE A CHANCE

Lyric by BILLY ROSE and E.Y. HARBURG
Music by HAROLD ARLEN

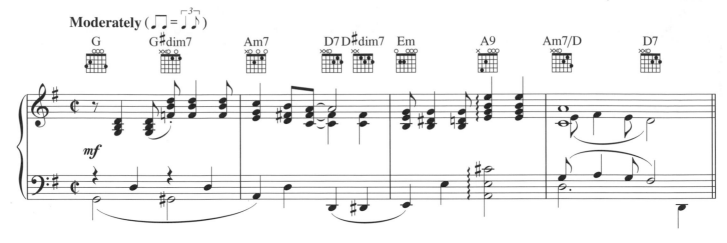

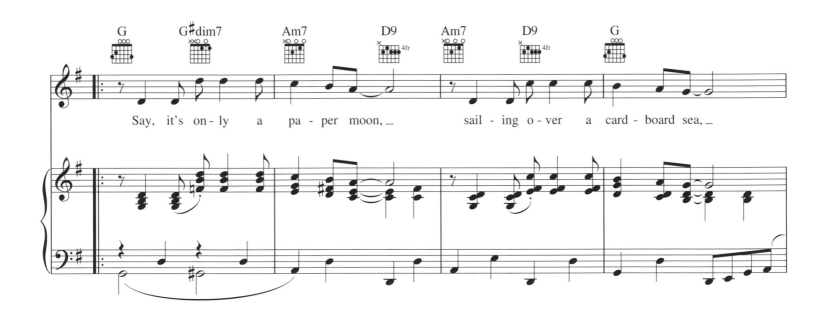

Say, it's on-ly a pa-per moon, ___ sail-ing o-ver a card-board sea, ___

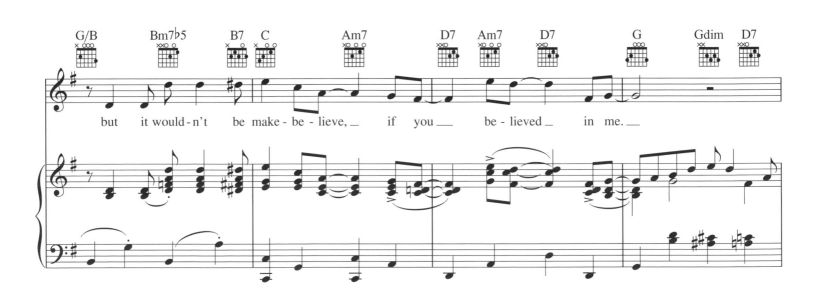

but it would-n't be make-be-lieve, ___ if you ___ be-lieved ___ in me. ___

Yes, it's on-ly a can-vas sky, hang-ing o-ver a mus-lin tree,

but it would-n't be make-be-lieve, if you be-lieved in me. With-

out your love, it's a hon-ky-tonk pa-rade. With-out your

146

IT'S THE TALK OF THE TOWN

Words by MARTY SYMES and AL NEIBURG
Music by JERRY LIVINGSTON

JERSEY BOUNCE

Words by ROBERT WRIGHT
Music by BOBBY PLATTER, TINY BRADSHAW,
ED JOHNSON and ROBERT WRIGHT

LET'S GET AWAY FROM IT ALL

Words and Music by TOM ADAIR
and MATT DENNIS

LILLI MARLENE

German Lyric by HANS LEIP
English Lyric by TOMMIE CONNOR
Music by NORBERT SCHULTZE

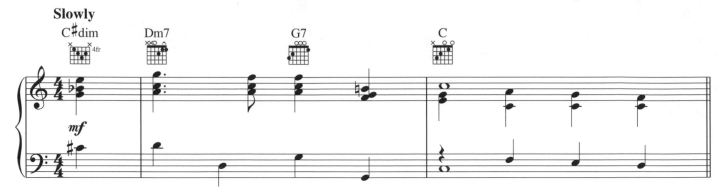

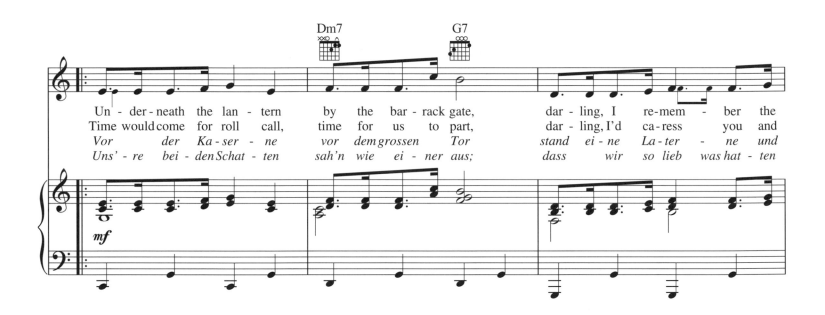

Un - der - neath the lan - tern by the bar - rack gate,
Time would come for roll call, time for us to part,
Vor der Ka - ser - ne vor dem grossen Tor

dar - ling, I re - mem - ber the
dar - ling, I'd ca - ress you and
stand ei - ne La - ter - ne und

way you used to wait. 'Twas there that you whis - pered ten - der - ly that
press you to my heart. And there 'neath that far - off lan - tern light I'd
steht sie noch da - ror, So woll'n wir da uns wie - der - sehn, bei
sah man gleich da - raus. Und al - le Leu - te soll'n es sehn wenn

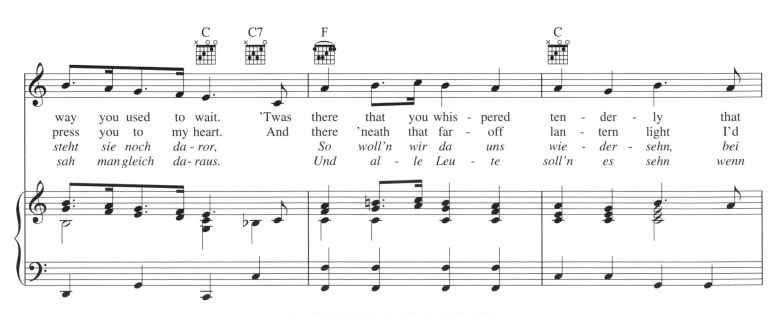

Un - s' - re bei - den Schat - ten sah'n wie ei - ner aus;
dass wir so lieb was hat - ten

you lov'd me, you'd al - ways be)
hold you tight, we'd kiss "good - night,") my Lil - li of the lamp - light, my
der La - ter - ne woll'n wir steh'n)
wir bei der La - ter - ne steh'n) *wie einst Lil - li Mar - leen,* wie

own Lil - li Mar - lene.
einst Lil - li Mar - leen.

Or - ders came for sail - ing some-where o - ver there, all con - fined to bar - racks was
Rest - ing in a bil - let just be-hind the line, e - ven tho' we're part - ed your
Schon rief der Po - sten: sie bla - sen Za - pfen sheich; es kann drei Ta - ge ko - sten! Ka - me
Dei - ne Schrit - te kennt sie, dei - nen zie - ren Gang, al - le A - bendbrennt sie
Aus dem stil - lin Rau - me, aus der Er - de Grund hebt mich wie im Trau - me

LULLABY OF THE LEAVES

Words by JOE YOUNG
Music by BERNICE PETKERE

Rus-tling of the leaves used to be my lull-a-by,

MAIRZY DOATS

Words and Music by MILTON DRAKE,
AL HOFFMAN and JERRY LIVINGSTON

Lightly

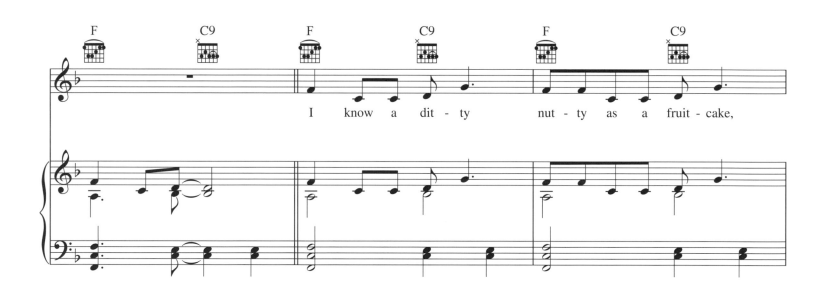

I know a dit-ty nut-ty as a fruit-cake,

goof-y as a goon and sil-ly as a loon. Some call it pret-ty,

MOONLIGHT IN VERMONT

Words and Music by JOHN BLACKBURN
and KARL SUESSDORF

MANHATTAN
from the Broadway Musical THE GARRICK GAIETIES

Words by LORENZ HART
Music by RICHARD RODGERS

We'll set - tle down right here in town.

We'll have Man - hat - tan, the Bronx and Stat - en Is - land too; _____ It's love - ly
We'll go to Green - wich where mod - ern men itch to be free; _____ And Bowl - ing
We'll go to Yon - kers where true love con - quers in the wilds; _____ And starve to -
We'll have Man - hat - tan, the Bronx and Stat - en Is - land too; _____ We'll try to

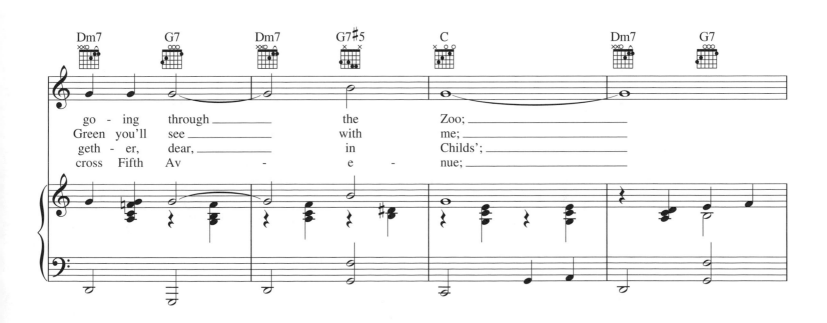

go - ing through _____ the Zoo; _____
Green you'll see _____ with me; _____
geth - er, dear, _____ in Childs'; _____
cross Fifth Av - e - nue; _____

It's ver-y fan-cy on old De-lan-cey Street, you know; _____ The sub-way
We'll bathe at Brigh-ton the fist you'll fright-en when you're in; _____ Your bath-ing
We'll go to Co-ney and eat bo-lo-gna on a roll; _____ In Cen-tral
As black as on-yx we'll find the Bron-nix Park Ex-press; _____ Our Flat-bush

charms us so, _____ when balm-y breez-es blow to and fro; And tell me what street
suit so thin _____ will make the shell-fish grin fin to fin; I'd like to take a
Park, we'll stroll _____ where our first kiss we stole, soul to soul; And for some high fare
flat, I guess _____ will be a great suc-cess. More or less; A short va-ca-tion

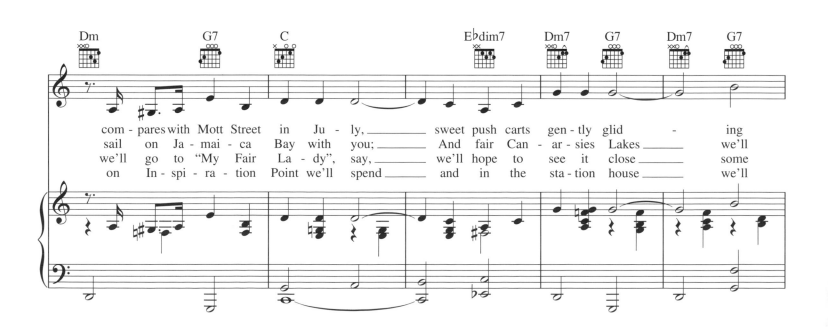

com-pares with Mott Street in Ju-ly, _____ sweet push carts gen-tly glid-ing
sail on Ja-mai-ca Bay with you; _____ And fair Can-ar-sies Lakes _____ we'll
we'll go to "My Fair La-dy", say, _____ we'll hope to see it close _____ some
on In-spi-ra-tion Point we'll spend _____ and in the sta-tion house _____ we'll

The great big cit - y's a won - drous toy just
view. The cit - y's bus - tle can - not de - stroy the
day. The cit - y's clam - or can nev - er spoil the
end. But Civ - ic Vir - tue can - not de - stroy the

made for a girl and boy.
dreams of a girl and boy.
dreams of a boy and goil.
dreams of a girl and boy.

We'll turn Man - hat - tan in - to an isle of

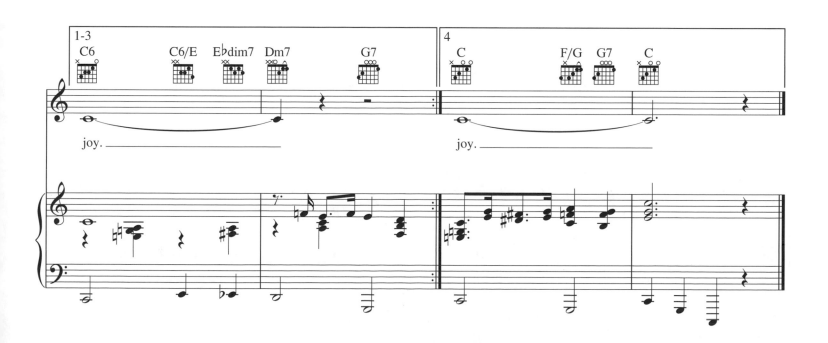

joy.

joy.

MARIE

from the Motion Picture THE AWAKENING

Words and Music by
IRVING BERLIN

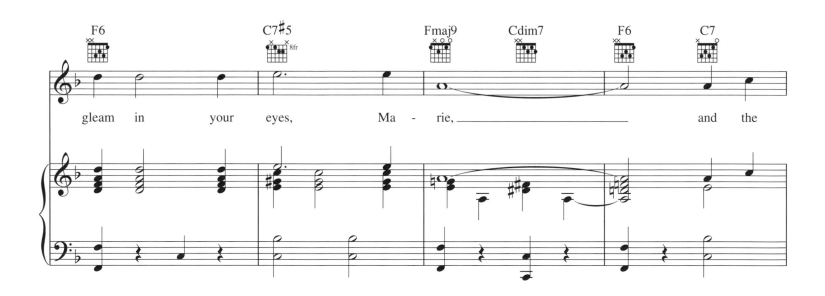

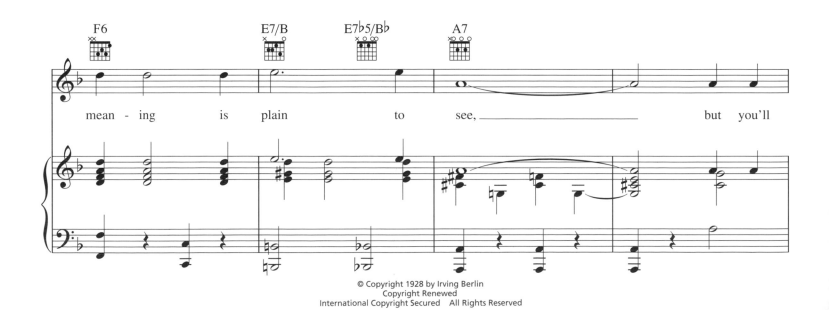

MOONGLOW

Words and Music by WILL HUDSON,
EDDIE DE LANGE and IRVING MILLS

(There Ought to Be A)
MOONLIGHT SAVING TIME

Words and Music by IRVING KAHAL
and HARRY RICHMAN

MY HEART BELONGS TO DADDY

from LEAVE IT TO ME

Words and Music by
COLE PORTER

heart be - longs __ to Dad - dy, Da - da, da - da - da, da - da - da -

ad! So I want to warn __ you, lad - die, though I

know you're per - fect - ly swell, that my heart be - longs __ to

Dad - dy _____ 'cause my Dad - dy, he treats it so well. While well.

NEVERTHELESS
(I'm in Love with You)

Words and Music by BERT KALMAR
and HARRY RUBY

OH JOHNNY, OH JOHNNY, OH!

Words by ED ROSE
Music by ABE OLMAN

OLD DEVIL MOON

from FINIAN'S RAINBOW

Words by E.Y. "YIP" HARBURG
Music by BURTON LANE

OPUS ONE

Words and Music by
SY OLIVER

Moderate Jump tempo

I'm wrack-in' my brain, to think of a name, _ to give to this tune, so Per-ry can croon, _ and may-be ol' Bing will give it a fling, _ and that-'ll start ev-'ry-one hum-min' the thing. _ The

PAPER DOLL

Words and Music by
JOHNNY S. BLACK

Slowly

I guess I've had a mil-lion dolls or more; I guess I've played the doll game o'er and o'er. I just quar-reled with Sue, __ that's why I'm blue; __ she's gone a-way and left me just like all dolls do. I'll

POLKA DOTS AND MOONBEAMS

Words by JOHNNY BURKE
Music by JIMMY VAN HEUSEN

A coun-try dance was be-ing held in a gar-den, I felt a bump and heard an "Oh, beg your par-don." Sud-den-ly I saw pol-ka dots and moon-beams all a-round a pug-nosed dream. The mu-sic start-ed and was

PENNIES FROM HEAVEN

from PENNIES FROM HEAVEN

Words by JOHN BURKE
Music by ARTHUR JOHNSTON

POINCIANA
(Song of the Tree)

Words by BUDDY BERNIER
Music by NAT SIMON

PUT YOUR ARMS
AROUND ME, HONEY

Words by JUNIE McREE
Music by ALBERT VON TILZER

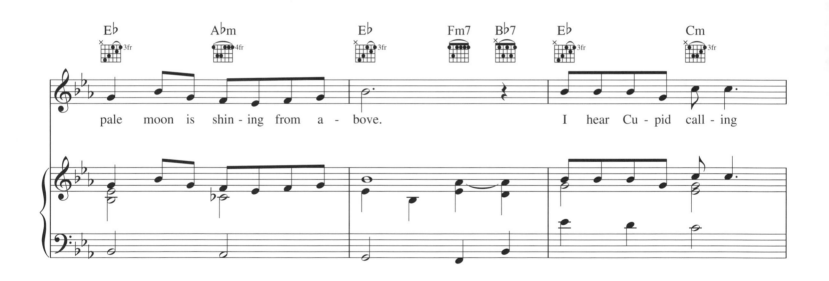

SLEEPY LAGOON

Words by JACK LAWRENCE
Music by ERIC COATES

A sleep-y la-goon, a trop-i-cal moon, and two on an is-land, _____ a sleep-y la-goon, and two hearts in tune, in some lull-a-bye-land. _____ The fi-re-flies'

spell, as night-in-gales tell of ros-es and dew. _____ The mem-o-ry of this mo-ment of love will haunt me for-ev-er. _____ A trop-i-cal moon, a sleep-y la-goon and

you. A sleep-y la- you. _____

RED SAILS IN THE SUNSET

Words by JIMMY KENNEDY
Music by HUGH WILLIAMS (WILL GROSZ)

SHOO FLY PIE AND APPLE PAN DOWDY

Words by SAMMY GALLOP
Music by GUY WOOD

SOMEBODY ELSE IS TAKING MY PLACE

Words and Music by DICK HOWARD,
BOB ELLSWORTH and RUSS MORGAN

Slowly, with expression

F7   B♭   G7   C7

smile on your face. Lit - tle you care for vows that you

F7   B♭

made. Lit - tle you care how much I have paid.

E♭   B♭   G7   C7

My heart is ach - ing, my heart is break - ing, for some - bod - y's

F7 E♭ F7   1. B♭ B♭dim7 Cm7 F7   2. B♭ E♭6 E♭m6 B♭

tak - ing my place.   place.

STARDUST

Words by MITCHELL PARISH
Music by HOAGY CARMICHAEL

STOMPIN' AT THE SAVOY

Words and Music by BENNY GOODMAN,
EDGAR SAMPSON, CHICK WEBB and ANDY RAZAF

A STRING OF PEARLS
from THE GLENN MILLER STORY

Words by EDDIE DE LANGE
Music by JERRY GRAY

SUNDAY, MONDAY OR ALWAYS

Words by JOHNNY BURKE
Music by JIMMY VAN HEUSEN

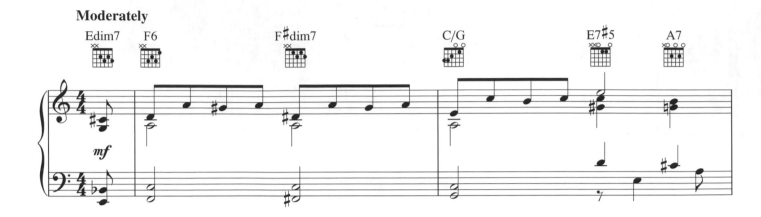

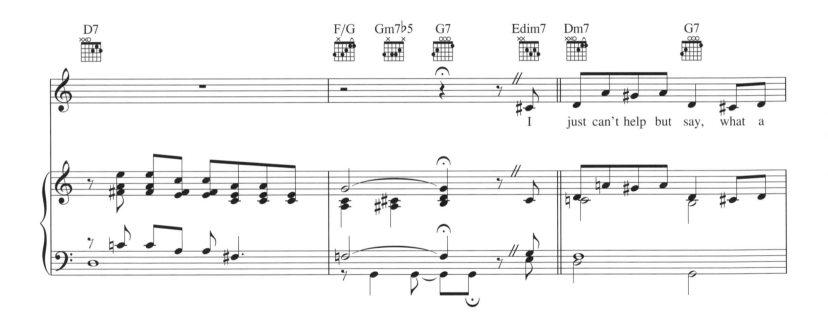

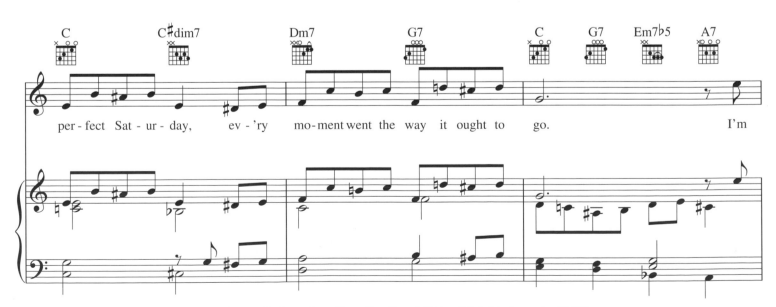

Sun-day, Mon-day, or al-ways. No need to tell me now what

makes the world go 'round, when at the sight of you my

heart be-gins to pound and pound. And what am I to do? Can't I be with you

Sun-day, Mon-day, or al-ways? al-ways?

SUNRISE SERENADE

Lyric by JACK LAWRENCE
Music by FRANKIE CARLE

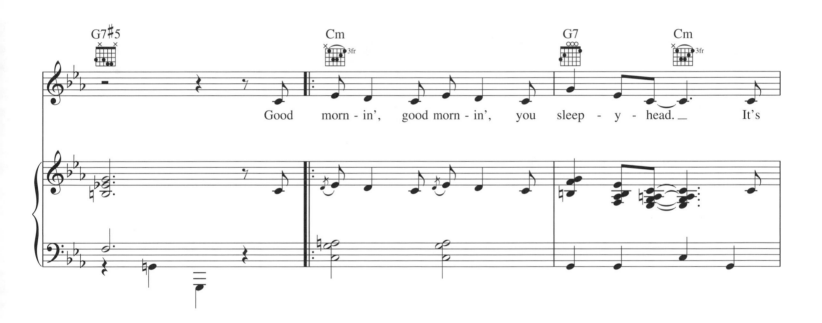

Good morn-in', good morn-in', you sleep-y-head. ___ It's

dawn-in', stop yawn-in', get out of that bed. ___ Say the air is soft as silk, ___ it's time to

SWEET SUE-JUST YOU

from RHYTHM PARADE

Words by WILL J. HARRIS
Music by VICTOR YOUNG

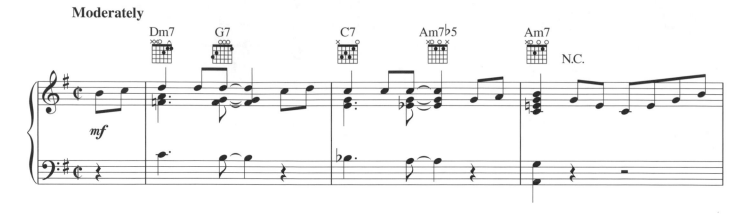

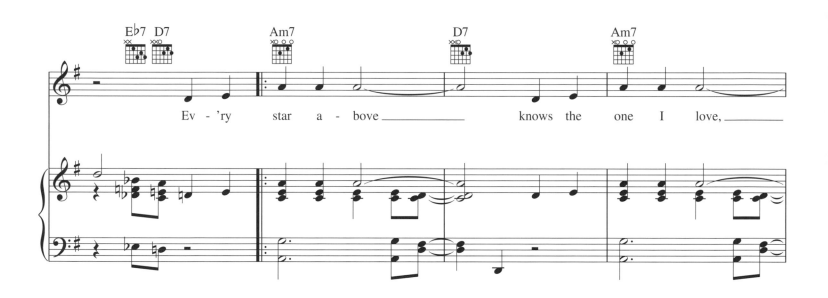

Ev - 'ry star a - bove _____ knows the one I love, _____

_____ sweet Sue, _____ just you. _____

'TAIN'T WHAT YOU DO
(It's the Way That Cha Do It)

Words and Music by SY OLIVER
and JAMES YOUNG

THERE ARE SUCH THINGS

Words and Music by STANLEY ADAMS,
ABEL BAER and GEORGE W. MEYER

THERE'S A SMALL HOTEL
from ON YOUR TOES

Words by LORENZ HART
Music by RICHARD RODGERS

THERE'LL BE SOME CHANGES MADE

from ALL THAT JAZZ

Words by BILLY HIGGINS
Music by W. BENTON OVERSTREET

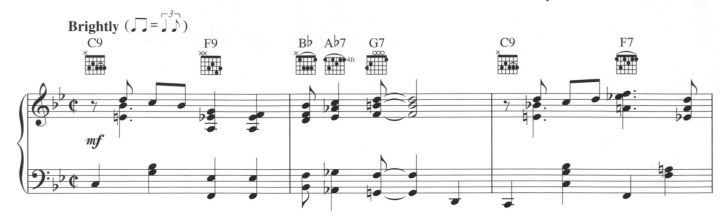

For there's a change in the weath - er, there's a change in the sea, ___

so from now on there'll be a change in me. ___ My walk will be dif - f'rent, my

THESE FOOLISH THINGS
(Remind Me of You)

Words by HOLT MARVELL
Music by JACK STRACHEY

THE THINGS WE DID LAST SUMMER

Words by SAMMY CAHN
Music by JULE STYNE

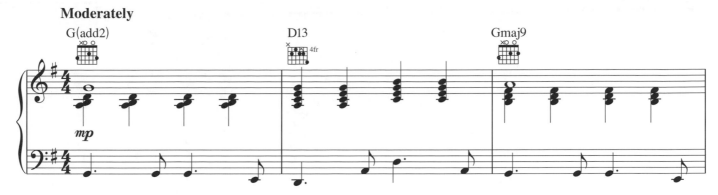

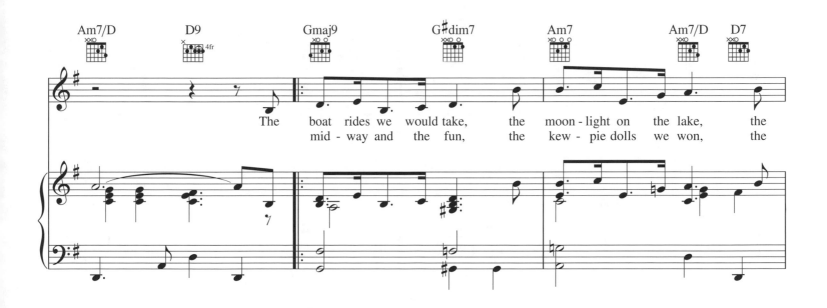

The boat rides we would take, the moon-light on the lake, the
mid - way and the fun, the kew - pie dolls we won, the

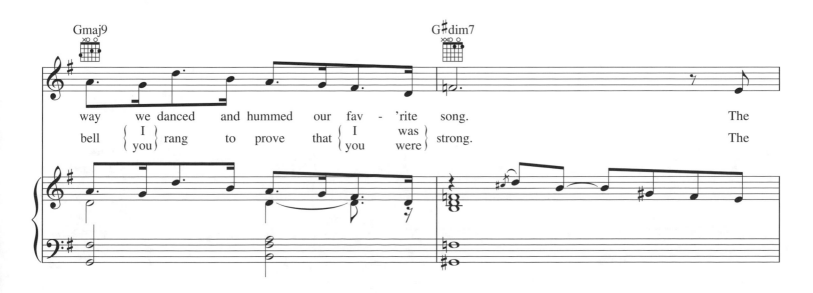

way we danced and hummed our fav - 'rite song. The
bell {I / you} rang to prove that {I was / you were} strong. The

THREE LITTLE FISHIES
(Itty Bitty Poo)

Words and Music by
SAXIE DOWELL

Brightly

1. *Down in the mead-ow in a lit-tle bit-ty pool swam three lit-tle fish-ies and a ma-ma fish-ie, too.*
   Down in de med-dy in a it-ty bit-ty poo fam fee it-ty fit-ty and a ma-ma fit-ty, foo.

2. *"Stop," said the ma-ma fish-ie, "or you will get lost." The three lit-tle fish-ies did-n't wan-na be bossed. The*
   "Top," ted de ma-ma fit-ty, "Or oo ill det ost." De fee it-ty fit-ty din-na an-na be bossed. De

3.,4. (See additional lyrics)

"Swim," said the ma-ma fish-ie, "Swim if you can," and they swam and they swam all o-ver the dam.
"Fim," fed de ma-ma fit-ty, "Fim if oo tan," and dey fam and dey fam all o-ver de dam.
three lit-tle fish-ies went off on a spree, and they swam and they swam right out to the sea.
fee it-ty fit-ty ent off on a spwee, and dey fam and dey fam ight out to de fee.

8vb

Boop boop dit - tem dat - tem what - tem. Chu! Boop boop dit - tem dat - tem what - tem. Chu!
Boop boop dit - tem dat - tem what - tem. Chu! Boop boop dit - tem dat - tem what - tem. Chu!

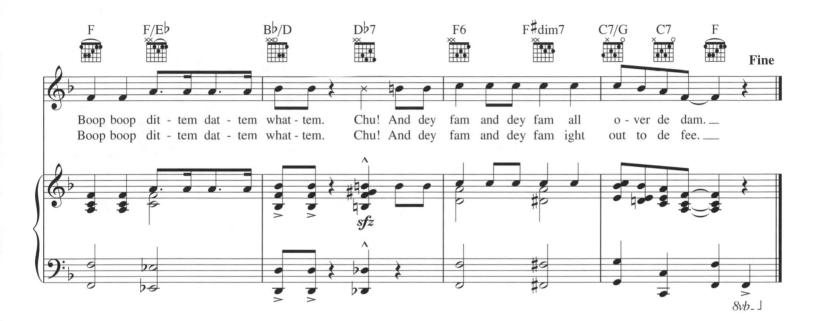

Boop boop dit - tem dat - tem what - tem. Chu! And dey fam and dey fam all o - ver de dam.
Boop boop dit - tem dat - tem what - tem. Chu! And dey fam and dey fam ight out to de fee.

Interlude

D.S. al Fine

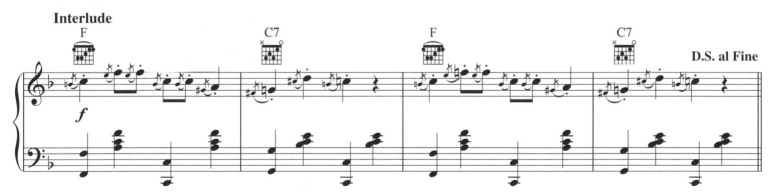

Additional Lyrics

3. "Whee!" yelled the little fishies, "Here's a lot of fun.
We'll swim in the sea till the day is done."
They swam and they swam and it was a lark,
Till all of a sudden they saw a shark!

"Whee!" 'elled de itty fitties, "Ears a wot of fun.
Ee'll fim in de fee ill de day is un."
Dey fam and dey fam and it was a wark,
Till aw of a tudden dey taw a tark!

Boop boop dittem dattem whattem. Chu!
Boop boop dittem dattem whattem. Chu!
Boop boop dittem dattem whattem. Chu!
Till aw of a tudden dey taw a tark!

4. "Help!" cried the little fishies, "Gee! Look at all the whales!"
And quick as they could they turned on their tails.
And back to the pool in the meadow they swam,
And they swam and they swam back over the dam.

"He'p!" tied de itty fitties, "Dee! Ook at all de fales!"
And twit as dey tood dey turned on deir tails.
And bat to de poo in de meddy dey fam,
And dey fam and dey fam bat over de dam.

Boop boop dittem dattem whattem. Chu!
Boop boop dittem dattem whattem. Chu!
Boop boop dittem dattem whattem. Chu!
And dey fam and dey fam bat over de dam.

TILL THE END OF TIME

from TILL THE END OF TIME

(Based on Chopin's Polonaise)
Words and Music by BUDDY KAYE
and TED MOSSMAN

Slowly and very expressively

I wished up-on a star for some-one to share what each day would bring.

And you, my dar-ling, are that some-one meant for me to cling to till the

end of time. _____ Long as stars are in the blue, _____ long as

UNDER A BLANKET OF BLUE

Words by MARTY SYMES and AL J. NEIBURG
Music by JERRY LIVINGSTON

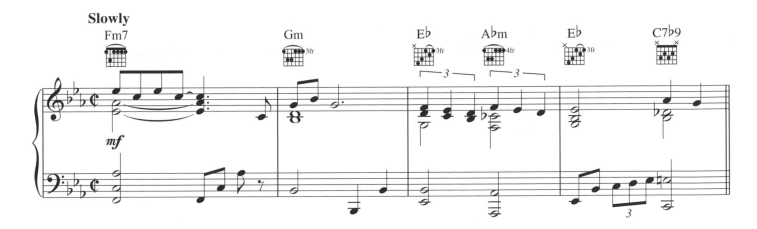

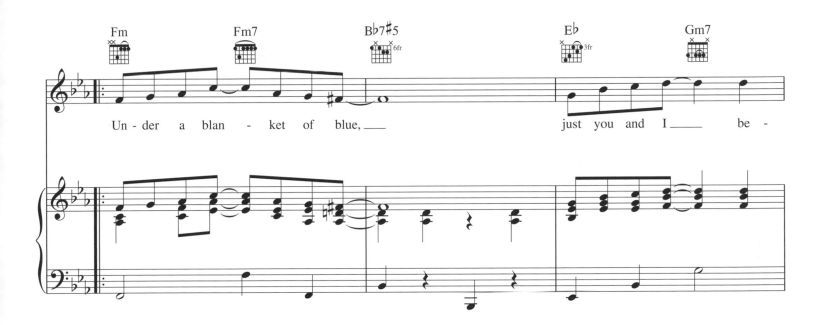

Un-der a blan-ket of blue, ___ just you and I ___ be-

neath the stars, wrapped in the arms ___ of sweet ro-mance, the night is ours. ___

TUXEDO JUNCTION

Words by BUDDY FEYNE
Music by ERSKINE HAWKINS,
WILLIAM JOHNSON and JULIAN DASH

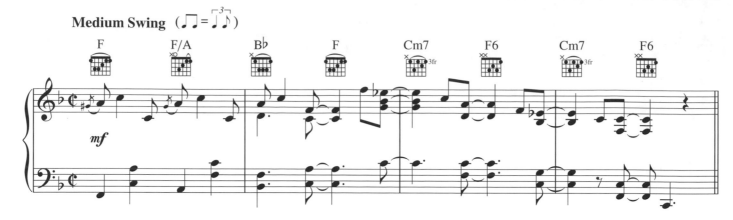

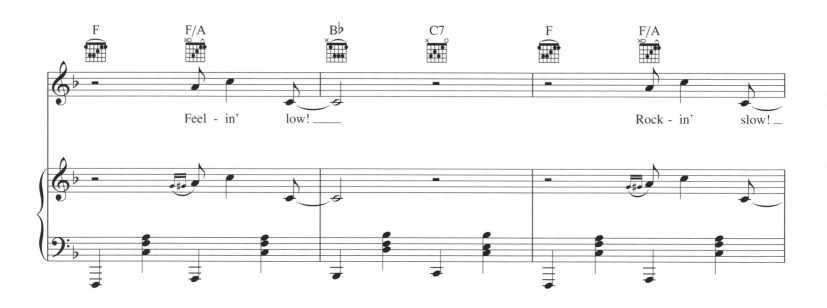

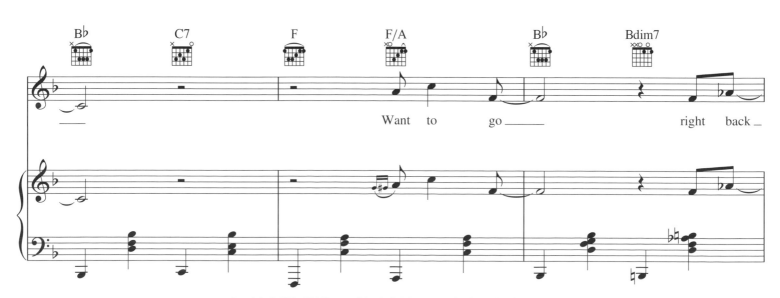

THE VARSITY DRAG

from GOOD NEWS

Words and Music by B.G. DeSYLVA,
LEW BROWN and RAY HENDERSON

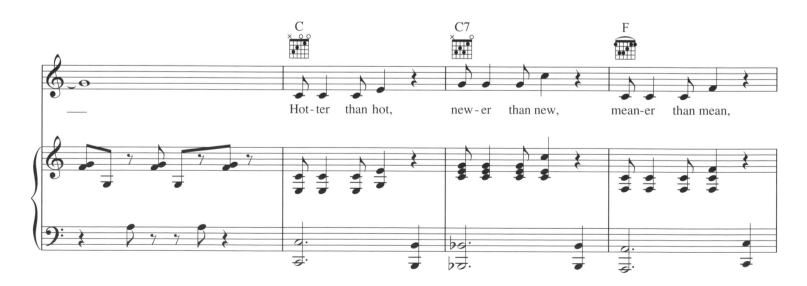

blu - er than blue.   Gets as much ap - plause as wav - ing the   Flag!

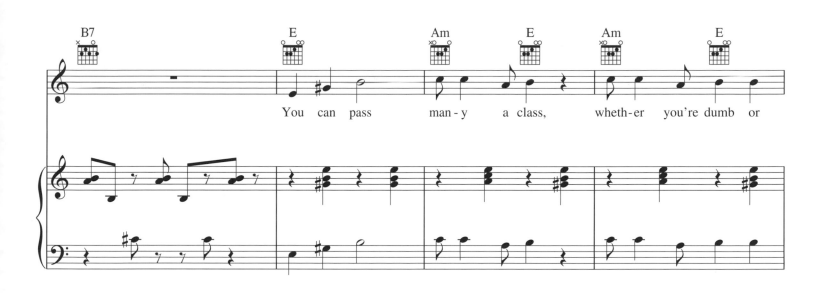

You can pass   man - y   a class,   wheth - er you're dumb or

wise,   if you all   an - swer   the call,   when your pro - fes - sor

cries, "Ev - 'ry - bod - y down on the heels, up on the toes.

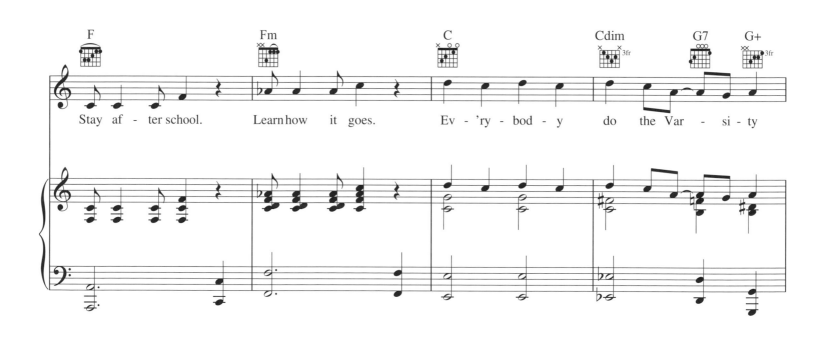

Stay af - ter school. Learn how it goes. Ev - 'ry - bod - y do the Var - si - ty

Drag." _____ Drag." _____

WHERE THE BLUE OF THE NIGHT
(Meets the Gold of the Day)

Lyric and Music by FRED E. AHLERT,
BING CROSBY and ROY TURK

Where the blue of the night meets the gold of the day some-one waits for me. _____ And the

G   B7   C6

gold of her hair crowns the blue of her

Am7♭5   G   D7

eyes like a ha - lo, ten - der -

G   G7   C

ly.   If on - ly

D7   Cm G   G7

I could see her,   oh, how

YES INDEED

Words and Music by
SY OLIVER

YOU BROUGHT A NEW KIND OF LOVE TO ME

from the Paramount Picture THE BIG POND
from NEW YORK, NEW YORK

Words and Music by SAMMY FAIN,
IRVING KAHAL and PIERRE NORMAN

YOU TURNED THE TABLES ON ME

Words by SIDNEY MITCHELL
Music by LOUIS ALTER

Moderate Ballad

I used to be the ap-ple of your eye, I had you with me ev-'ry day.

But now when-ev-er you are pass-ing by you're al-ways look-ing the oth-er way. It's lit-tle things like this that

YOU'D BE SO NICE TO COME HOME TO

from SOMETHING TO SHOUT ABOUT

Words and Music by
COLE PORTER

Moderately slow, with feeling

It's not that you're fair-er, than a lot of girls just as pleas-in', that I doff my hat as a wor-ship-per at your shrine. ___ It's

YOU'RE THE CREAM IN MY COFFEE

from HOLD EVERYTHING

Words and Music by B.G. DeSYLVA,
LEW BROWN and RAY HENDERSON

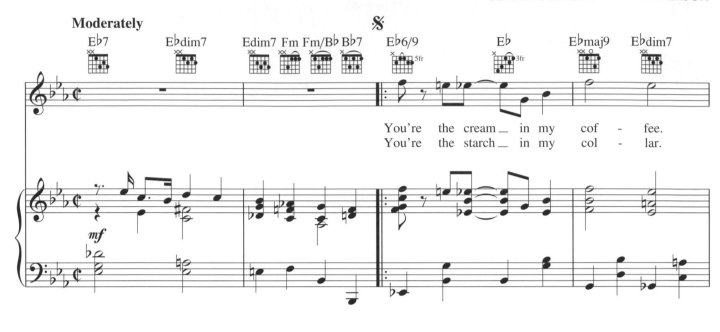

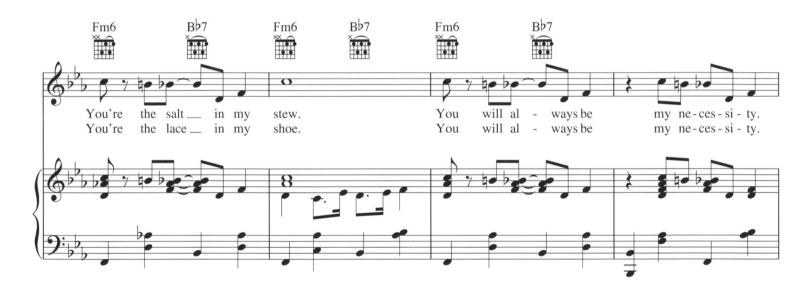

WILLOW WEEP FOR ME

Words and Music by
ANN RONELL

Gm G7 Cm B♭7 A♭ D7 D+
hide her star - ry light, So none will find me sigh - ing and cry - ing all a - lone. Oh,
G D9♯5 G D9♯5 G Em Bm
weep - ing wil - low tree, weep in sym - pa - thy, Bend your branch - es down a - long the ground
Em C9 D+
and cov - er me. When the shad - ows fall, bend, oh wil - low, and weep for me.
G D7♯5
1 G D7♯5
2 G
rit.